THE COTTAGE COOK
&
THE SUNDAY SCHOOL

The Cottage Cook

Mrs. Jones Cheap Dishes; Showing the Way to Do Much Good with Little Money

The Sunday School

The Manner in Which Mrs. Jones Set Up Her School

BY
HANNAH MORE

CURIOSMITH
MINNEAPOLIS

Published by Curiosmith.
Minneapolis, Minnesota.
Internet: curiosmith.com.

The Cottage Cook previously published by MARSHALL
PR., WHITE, HAZZARD, ELDER in 1796, as part of the
Cheap Repository Tracts.

The Sunday School previously published by MARSHALL
PR., WHITE, HAZZARD, ELDER in 1797, as part of the
Cheap Repository Tracts.

Footnotes marked "original footnote" are footnotes
from the source text. All other footnotes were added to
this edition by the publisher.

Scripture text unless otherwise indicated is from *The
Holy Bible*, King James Version.

Supplementary content, book layout and cover design:
Copyright © 2016 Charles J. Doe.

ISBN 9781941281758

CONTENTS

The Cottage Cook

Mrs. Jones's Cheap Dishes

Mrs. Jones was the widow of a great merchant. She was liberal to the poor, as far as giving them money went; but as she was too much taken up with the world, she did not spare so much of her time and thoughts about doing good as she ought; so that her money was often ill bestowed. In the late troubles, Mr. Jones, who had lived in an expensive manner, failed; and he took his misfortunes so much to heart, that he fell sick and died. Mrs. Jones retired, on a very narrow income, to the small village of Weston, where she

seldom went out, except to church.
Though a pious woman, she was too
apt to indulge her sorrow; and though
she did not neglect to read and pray,
yet she gave up a great part of her time
to melancholy thoughts, and grew
quite inactive. She well knew how sin-
ful it would be for her to seek a remedy for her grief in worldly pleasures,
which is a way many people take to
cure afflictions; but she was not aware
how wrong it was to weep away that
time which might have been better
spent in drying the tears of others.

It was happy for her, that Mr.
Simpson, the vicar of Weston, was a
pious man.[1] One Sunday he happened

---

1 Weston, near Bath, where all that
is related here, and in the subsequent
narratives connected with this story,
actually occurred; and became the model
of imitation in other places. See the

to preach on the good Samaritan. It was a charity sermon, and there was a collection at the door. He called on Mrs. Jones after church, and found her in tears. She told him she had been much moved by his discourse, and she wept because she had so little to give to the plate; for though she felt very keenly for the poor in these dear times, yet she could not assist them.

"Indeed, sir," added she, "I never so much regretted the loss of my fortune as this afternoon, when you bade us 'go and do likewise.'"

"You do not," replied Mr. Simpson "enter into the spirit of our Savior's parable, if you think you cannot go and do likewise without being rich. In the case of the Samaritan, you may

First Report of the Ladies' Society for the Education and Employment of the Female Poor, 1805.—ED. *(Original footnote)*

observe, that charity was bestowed more by kindness, and care, and medicine, than by money. You, madam, were as much concerned in the duties inculcated in my sermon, as Sir John with his great estate; and, to speak plainly, I have been sometimes surprised that you should not put yourself in the way of being more useful."

"Sir," said Mrs. Jones, "I am grown shy of the poor since I have nothing to give them."

"Nothing, madam!" replied the clergyman. "Do you call your time, your talents, your kind offices, nothing? Doing good does not so much depend on the riches, as on the heart and the will. The servant who improved his two talents was equally commended by his lord with him who had ten; and it was not poverty, but selfish indolence, which drew down so severe a condemnation on him who had only one. It is by our conformity to Christ, that we must prove ourselves Christians. You, madam, are not called upon to work miracles, nor to preach the gospel; yet you may, in your measure and degree, resemble your Savior by *going about* and *doing good*. A plain Christian, who has sense and leisure, by his pious exertions and prudent zeal, may, in a subordinate way, be helping on the cause of religion, as well as of charity; and greatly promote, by his exertions and example, the labors of the parish minister. The generality, it is true, have but an under-part to act; but to all, God assigns some part, and he will require of all whose lot is not very laborious, that they not only work out their own salvation, but that they promote the cause of religion, and the comfort and salvation of others.

"To those who would undervalue works of mercy as evidences of piety, I would suggest a serious attention to the solemn appeal which the Savior of the world makes, in that awful representation of the day of judgment contained in the twenty-fifth chapter of Matthew, both to those who have neglected and to those who have performed such works; performed them, I mean, on right principles. With what a gracious condescension does he promise to accept the smallest kindness done to his suffering members for his sake! You, madam, I will venture to say, might do more good than the richest man in the parish could do by merely giving his money. Instead of sitting here, brooding over your misfortunes, which are past remedy, bestir yourself to find out ways of doing much good with little money; or even without any money at all. You have lately studied economy for yourself; instruct your poor neighbors in that important art. They want it almost as much as they want money. You have influence with the few rich persons in the parish; exert that influence. Betty, my housekeeper, shall assist you in any thing in which she can be useful. Try this for one year, and if you then tell me that you should have better shown your love to God and man, and been a happier woman, had you continued gloomy and inactive, I shall be much surprised, and shall consent to your resuming your present way of life."

The sermon and this discourse together, made so deep an impression on Mrs. Jones, that she formed a new plan of life, and set about it at once, as every body does who is in earnest. Her chief aim was the happiness of her

poor neighbors in the next world; but
she was also very desirous to promote
their present comfort; and indeed the
kindness she showed to their bodily
wants gave her such an access to their
houses and hearts, as made them better disposed to receive religious counsel and instruction. Mrs. Jones was
much respected by all the rich persons
in Weston, who had known her in her
prosperity. Sir John was thoughtless,
lavish, and indolent; the squire was
over-frugal, but active, sober, and not
ill-natured. Sir John loved pleasure;
the squire loved money. Sir John was
one of those popular sort of people
who get much praise, and yet do little
good; who subscribe with equal readi-
ness to a cricket-match or a charity-
school; who take it for granted, that
the poor are to be indulged with bell-
ringing and bonfires, and to be made

drunk at Christmas; this, Sir John called being kind to them; but he thought it was folly to teach them, and madness to think of reforming them. He was, however, always ready to give his guinea; but I question whether he would have given up his hunting and his gaming, to have cured every grievance in the land. He had that sort of constitutional good-nature which, if he had lived much within sight of misery, would have led him to be liberal; but he had that selfish love of ease, which prompted him to give to undeserving objects, rather than be at the pains to search out the deserving. He neither discriminated between the degrees of distress, nor the characters of the distressed. His idea of charity was, that a rich man should occasionally give a little of his superfluous wealth to the first object that occurred;

but he had no conception that it was his duty so to husband his wealth, and limit his expenses, as to supply a regular fund for established charity. And this utmost stretch of his benevolence never led him to suspect that he was called to abridge himself in the most idle article of indulgence, for a purpose foreign to his own personal enjoyment. On the other hand, the squire would assist Mrs. Jones in any of her plans, if it cost him nothing; so she showed her good sense by never asking Sir John for advice, or the squire for subscriptions; and by this prudence gained the full support of both.

Mrs. Jones resolved to spend two or three days in a week in getting acquainted with the state of the parish, and she took care never to walk out without a few little good books in her pocket, to give away. This, though a cheap, is a most important act of charity: it has various uses; it furnishes the poor with religious knowledge, which they have so few ways of obtaining; it counteracts the wicked designs of those who have taught us at least one lesson, by their zeal in the dispersion of *wicked* books—I mean, the lesson of vigilance and activity; and it is the best introduction for any useful conversation which the giver of the book may wish to introduce.

She found, that among the numerous wants she met with, no small share was owing to bad management, or to imposition: she was struck with the small size of the loaves. Wheat was now not very dear, and she was sure a good deal of blame rested with the baker. She sent for a shilling loaf to the next great town, where the mayor often sent to the baker's shops to see that the bread was proper weight. She weighed her town loaf against her country loaf, and found the latter two pounds lighter than it ought to be. This was not the sort of grievance to carry to Sir John; but luckily the squire was also a magistrate, and it was quite in his way; for though he could not give, yet he would counsel, calculate, contrive, reprimand, and punish. He told her he could remedy the evil, if some one would lodge an information against the baker; but that there was no act of justice which he found it so difficult to accomplish.

The Informer

She dropped in on the blacksmith. He was at dinner. She inquired if his bread was good.

"Ay, good enough, mistress, for you

see it is as white as your cap, if we had but more of it. Here's a sixpenny loaf; you might take it for a penny roll!"

He then heartily cursed Crib the baker, and said he ought to be hanged. Mrs. Jones now told him what she had done; how she had detected the fraud, and assured him the evil should be redressed on the morrow, provided he would appear and inform.

"I inform!" said he, with a shocking oath, "hang an informer! I scorn the office."

"You are nice in the wrong place," replied Mrs. Jones; "for you don't scorn to abuse the baker, nor to be in a passion, nor to swear, though you scorn to redress a public injury, and to increase your children's bread. Let me tell you, there is nothing in which you ignorant people mistake more than in your notions about informers.

Informing is a lawful way of obtaining redress; and though it is a mischievous and a hateful thing to go to a justice about every trifling matter, yet laying an information on important occasions, without malice, or bitterness of any kind, is what no honest man ought to be ashamed of. The shame is to commit the offense, not to inform against it. I, for my part, should perhaps do right, if I not only informed against Crib, for making light bread, but against you, for swearing at him."

"Well, but, madam," said the smith, a little softened, "don't you think it a sin and a shame to turn informer?"

"So far from it, that when a man's motives are good," said Mrs. Jones, "and in such clear cases as the present, I think it a duty and a virtue. If it is right that there should be laws, it must be right that they should be put in execution; but how can this be, if people will not inform the magistrates when they see the laws broken? I hope I shall always be afraid to be an offender against the laws, but not to be an informer in support of them. An informer *by trade* is commonly a knave. A rash, malicious, or passionate informer is a firebrand; but honest and prudent informers are almost as useful members of society as the judges of the land. If you continue in your present mind on this subject, do not you think that you will be answerable for the crimes you might have prevented by informing, and thus become a sort of accomplice of the villains who commit them?"

"Well, madam," said the smith, "I now see plainly enough that there is no shame in turning informer when my cause is good."

"And your *motive right;* always mind that," said Mrs. Jones.

Next day the smith attended; Crib was fined in the usual penalty; his light bread was taken from him, and given to the poor. The justices resolved henceforward to inspect the bakers in their district; and all of them, except Crib, and such as Crib, were glad of it; for honesty never dreads a trial. Thus had Mrs. Jones the comfort of seeing how useful people may be without expense; for if she could have given the poor fifty pounds, she would not have done them so great, or so lasting a benefit, as she did them in seeing their loaves restored to their lawful weight; and the true light in which she had put the business of *informing* was of no small use, in giving the neighborhood right views on that subject.

There were two shops in the

parish; but Mrs. Sparks, at the Cross, had not half so much custom as Wills, at the Sugar-loaf, though she sold her goods a penny in a shilling cheaper, and all agreed that they were much better. Mrs. Jones asked Mrs. Sparks the reason.

"Madam," said the shopkeeper, "Mr. Wills will give longer trust. Besides this, his wife keeps a shop on a Sunday morning while I am at church."

Mrs. Jones now reminded Mr. Simpson to read the king's proclamation against vice and immorality next Sunday at church; and prevailed on the squire to fine any one who should keep open-shop on a Sunday. This he readily undertook; for while Sir John thought it *good-natured* to connive at breaking the laws, the squire fell into the other extreme, of thinking that

the zealous enforcing of penal statutes
would stand in the stead of all religious
restraints. Mrs. Jones proceeded to put
the people in mind, that a shopkeeper
who would sell on a Sunday, would be
more likely to cheat them all the week,
than one who went to church.

She also labored hard to convince
them how much they would lessen
their distress, if they would contrive
to deal with Mrs. Sparks for ready
money, rather than with Wills on long
credit; those who listened to her found
their circumstances far more comfort-
able at the year's end, while the rest,
tempted, like some of their betters, by
the pleasure of putting off the evil day
of payment, like them, at last found
themselves plunged in debt and distress. She took care to make a good use
of such instances in her conversation
with the poor, and, by perseverance,

she at length brought them so much to
her way of thinking, that Wills found
it to be his interest to alter his plan,
and sell his goods on as good terms,
and as short credit, as Mrs. Sparks sold
hers. This completed Mrs. Jones's success; and she had the satisfaction of
having put a stop to three or four great
evils in the parish of Weston, without
spending a shilling in doing it.

Patty Smart and Jenny Rose were
thought to be the two best managers in
the parish. They both told Mrs. Jones,
that the poor would get the coarse
pieces of meat cheaper, if the gentle
folks did not buy them for soups and
gravy. Mrs. Jones thought there was
reason in this; so away she went to Sir
John, the squire, the surgeon, the attorney, and the steward, the only persons
in the parish who could afford to buy
these costly things. She told them, that

if they would all be so good as to buy only prime pieces, which they could very well afford, the coarse and cheap joints would come more within the reach of the poor. Most of the gentry readily consented. Sir John cared not what his meat cost him, but told Mrs. Jones, in his gay way, that he would eat any thing, or give any thing, so that she would not tease him with long stories about the poor. The squire said, he should prefer vegetable soups, because they were cheaper; and the doctor preferred them because they were wholesomer. The steward chose to imitate the squire; and the attorney found it would be quite ungenteel to stand out. So gravy soups became very unfashionable in the parish of Weston; and I am sure, if rich people did but think a little on this subject, they would become as unfashionable in many other places.

When wheat grew cheaper, Mrs. Jones was earnest with the poor women to bake large brown loaves at home, instead of buying small white ones at the shop. Mrs. Betty had told her, that baking at home would be one step towards restoring the good old management. Only Betty Smart and Jenny Rose baked at home in the whole parish; and who lived so well as they did? Yet the general objection seemed reasonable. They could not bake without yeast, which often could not be had, as no one brewed except the great folks and the public-houses. Mrs. Jones found, however, that Patty and Jenny contrived to brew as well as to bake. She sent for these women, knowing that from them she could get truth and reason.

"How comes it," said she to them, "that you two are the only poor women in the parish who can afford to brew a small cask of beer? Your husbands have no better wages than other men."

"True, madam," said Patty, "but they never set foot in a public-house. I will tell you the truth. When I first married, our John went to the Checkers every night, and I had my tea and fresh butter twice a day at home. This slop, which consumed a deal of sugar, began to *rake* my stomach sadly, as I had neither meat nor milk; at last (I am ashamed to own it) I began to take a drop of gin, to quiet the pain; till, in time, I looked for my gin as regularly as for my tea. At last the gin, the ale-house, and the tea, began to make us both sick and poor, and I had like to have died with my first child. Parson Simpson then talked so finely to us on the subject of improper indulgences, that we resolved, by the grace of God, to turn over a new leaf; and I promised John, if he would give up the Checkers, I would break the gin bottle, and never drink tea in the afternoon, except on Sundays, when he was at home to drink it with me. We have kept our word, and both our eating and drinking, our health and our consciences, are better for it. Though meat is sadly dear, we can buy two pounds of fresh meat for less than one pound of fresh butter, and it gives five times the nourishment. And dear as malt is, I contrive to keep a drop of drink in the house for John; and John will make me drink half a pint with him every evening, and a pint a day when I am a nurse."

PUBLIC-HOUSES

As one good deed, as well as one bad one, brings on another, this

conversation set Mrs. Jones on inquir-
ing why so many ale-houses were
allowed. She did not choose to talk to
Sir John on this subject, who would
only have said, "Let them enjoy themselves, poor fellows; if they get drunk
now and then, they work hard." But
those who have this false good-nature
forget, that while the man is *enjoying
himself,* as it is called, his wife and
children are ragged and starving. True
Christian good-nature never indulges
one at the cost of many, but is kind
to all. The squire, who was a friend
to order, took up the matter. He consulted Mr. Simpson.

"The Lion," said he, "is necessary. It stands by the road-side: trav-
ellers must have a resting-place. As to
the Checkers and the Bell, they do no
good, but much harm."

Mr. Simpson had before made

many attempts to get the Checkers put
down; but, unluckily, it was Sir John's
own house, and kept by his late butler.
Not that Sir John valued the rent, but
he had a false kindness, which made
him support the cause of an old servant, though he knew he was a bad
man, and kept a disorderly house.
The squire, however, now took away
the license from the Bell. And a fray
happening soon after at the Checkers
(which was near the church), in time
of divine service, Sir John was obliged
to suffer the house to be put down
as a nuisance. You would not believe
how many poor families were able to
brew a little cask, when the tempta-
tion of those ale-houses was taken out
of their way. Mrs. Jones, in her evening
walks, had the pleasure to see many an
honest man drinking his wholesome
cup of beer by his own fire-side, his

rosy children playing about his knees, his clean, cheerful wife singing her youngest baby to sleep, rocking the cradle with her foot, while, with her hands, she was making a dumpling for her kind husband's supper. Some few, I am sorry to say, though I don't choose to name names, still preferred getting drunk once a week at the Lion, and drinking water at other times.—Thus Mrs. Jones, by a little exertion and per-severance, added to the temporal com-forts of a whole parish, and diminished its immorality and extravagance in the same proportion.

The good women, being now supplied with yeast from each oth-er's brewings, would have baked, but two difficulties still remained. Many of them had no ovens; for since the new bad management had crept in, many cottages have been built without this convenience. Fuel also was scarce at Weston. Mrs. Jones advised the building a large parish oven. Sir John subscribed, to be rid of her importunity; and the squire, because he thought every improvement in economy would reduce the poor's rate. It was soon accomplished; and to this oven, at a certain hour, three times a week, the elder children carried their loaves which their mothers had made at home, and paid a halfpenny, or a penny, according to their size, for the baking.

Mrs. Jones found that no poor women in Weston could buy a little milk, as the farmers' wives did not care to rob their dairies. This was a great distress, especially when the children were sick. So Mrs. Jones advised Mrs. Sparks, at the Cross, to keep a couple of cows, and sell out the milk by

half-penny-worths. She did so, and
found, that though this plan gave her
some additional trouble, she got full as
much by it, as if she had made cheese
and butter. She also sold rice at a cheap
rate; so that, with the help of the milk
and the public oven, a fine rice pud-
ding was to be had for a trifle.

Charity School for Servants

The girls' school, in the parish, was
fallen into neglect; for though many
would be subscribers, yet no one would
look after it. I wish this was the case
at Weston only: many schools have
come to nothing, and many parishes
are quite destitute of schools, because
too many gentry neglect to make it
a part of the duty of their grown-up
daughters to inspect the instruction of
the poor. It was not in Mr. Simpson's

way to see if girls were taught to work. The best clergyman cannot do every-thing. This is ladies' business. Mrs. Jones consulted her counsellor, Mrs. Betty, and they went every Friday to the school, where they invited moth-ers, as well as daughters to come, and learn to cut out to the best advantage. Mrs. Jones had not been bred to these things; but by means of Mrs. Cowper's excellent cutting-out book, she soon became mistress of the whole art. She not only had the girls taught to make and mend, but to wash and iron too. She also allowed the mother or eldest daughter of every family to come once a week, and learn how to dress *one cheap dish.* One Friday, which was cooking-day, who should pass by but the squire, with his gun and dogs? He looked into the school for the first time.

"Well, madam," said he, "what good are you doing here? What are your girls learning and earning? Where are your manufactures? Where is your spinning and your carding?"

"Sir," said she, "this is a small parish, and you know ours is not a manufacturing county; so that when these girls are women, they will not be much employed in spinning. We must, in the kind of good we attempt to do, consult the local genius of the place; I do not think it will answer to introduce spinning, for instance, in a country where it is quite new. However, we teach them a little of it, and still more of knitting, that they may be able to get up a small piece of household linen once a year, and provide the family with stockings, by employing the odds and ends of their time in these ways. But there is another manufacture,

which I am carrying on, and I know
of none within my own reach which is
so valuable."

"What can that be?" said the
squire.

*"To make good wives for working
men,"* said she. "Is not mine an excellent staple commodity? I am teaching
these girls the arts of industry and good
management. It is little encouragement
to an honest man to work hard all the
week, if his wages are wasted by a slat-
tern at home. Most of these girls will
probably become wives to the poor, or
servants to the rich; to such, the common arts of life are of great value: now,
as there is little opportunity for learning
these at the school-house, I intend to
propose that such gentry as have sober
servants shall allow one of these girls
to come and work in their families one
day in a week, when the housekeeper,

the cook, the house-maid, or the laundry-maid, shall be required to instruct them in their several department. This I conceive to be the best way of training good servants. They should serve this kind of regular apprenticeship to various sorts of labor. Girls who come out of charity-schools, where they have been employed in knitting, sewing, and reading, are not sufficiently prepared for hard and laborious employments. I do not in general approve of teaching charity children to write, for the same reason. I confine within very strict limits my plan of educating the poor. A thorough knowledge of religion, and of some of those coarser arts of life, by which the community may be best benefited, includes the whole stock of instruction, which, unless in very extraordinary cases, I would wish to bestow."

"What have you got on the fire, madam?" said the squire; "for your pot really smells as savory as if Sir John's French cook had filled it."

"Sir," replied Mrs. Jones, "I have lately got acquainted with Mrs. White, who has given us an account of her cheap dishes and nice cookery, in one of the Cheap Repository little books.[1] Mrs. Betty and I have made all her dishes, and very good they are; and we have got several others of our own. Every Friday we come here, and dress one. These good women see how it is done, and learn to dress it at their own houses. I take home part for my own dinner, and what is left I give to each in turn. I hope I have opened their eyes on a sad mistake they had got into—*that* we *think any thing is*

1   See the *Way to Plenty*, for a number of cheap receipts. *(Original footnote)*

good enough for the poor. Now, I do not think any thing good enough for the poor which is not clean, wholesome, and palatable; and what I myself would not cheerfully eat, if my circumstances required it."

"Pray, Mrs. Betty," said the squire, "oblige me with a basin of your soup." The squire found it so good after his walk, that he was almost sorry he had promised to buy no more legs of beef, and declared, that not one sheep's head should ever go to his kennel again. He begged his cook might have the receipt; and Mrs. Jones wrote it out for her. She has also been so obliging as to favor me with a copy of all her receipts. And as I hate all monopoly, and see no reason why such cheap, nourishing, and savory dishes should be confined to the parish of Weston, I print them, that all other parishes may have the

THE SQUIRE FOUND THE SOUP SO GOOD, HE
BEGGED HIS COOK MIGHT HAVE THE RECEIPT.

same advantage. Not only the poor, but all persons with small incomes, may be glad of them.

"Well, madam," said Mr. Simpson, who came in soon after, "which is best, to sit down and cry over our misfortunes, or to bestir ourselves to do our duty to the world?"

"Sir," replied Mrs. Jones, "I thank you for the useful lesson you have given me. You have taught me that an excessive indulgence of sorrow is not piety, but selfishness; that the best remedy for our own afflictions is to lessen the afflictions of others, and thus evidence our submission to the will of God, who perhaps sent these very trials to abate our own self-love, and to stimulate our exertions for the good of others. You have taught me that our time and talents are to be employed with zeal in God's service, if we wish for his favor here or hereafter; and that one great employment of those talents, which he requires, is the promotion of the present, and much more the future happiness of all around us. You have taught me that much good may be done with little money; and that the heart, the head, and the hands, are of some use, as well as the purse. I have also learned another lesson, which I hope not to forget, that Providence, in sending these extraordinary seasons of scarcity and distress, which we have lately twice experienced, has been pleased to overrule these trying events to the general good; for it has not only excited the rich to an increased liberality, as to actual contribution, but it has led them to get more acquainted with the local wants of their poorer brethren, and to interest themselves in their comfort; it has led to improved modes of economy, and to a more feeling kind of beneficence. Above, all, without abating any thing of a just subordination, it has brought the affluent to a nearer knowledge of the persons and characters of their indigent neighbors; it has literally brought 'the rich and poor to meet together'; and this I look upon to be one of the essential advantages attending Sunday schools also, where they are carried on upon true principles, and are sanctioned by the visits, as well as supported by the contributions of the wealthy."

May all who read this account of Mrs. Jones, and who are under the same circumstances, *go and do likewise!*

The Sunday School

I promised, in the "The Cottage Cook," to give some account of the manner in which Mrs. Jones set up her school. She did not much fear being able to raise the money; but money is of little use, unless some persons of sense and piety can be found to direct these institutions. Not that I would discourage those who set them up, even in the most ordinary manner, and from mere views of worldly policy. It is something gained to rescue children from idling away their Sabbath in the fields or the streets. It is no small thing to keep them from those tricks to which a day of leisure tempts the idle and the ignorant. It is something for them to be taught to read; it is much to be taught to read the Bible; and much, indeed, to be carried regularly to church. But all this is not enough. To bring these institutions to answer their highest end, can only be effected by God's blessing on the best-directed means, and choice of able teachers, and a diligent attention in some pious gentry to visit and inspect the schools.

ON RECOMMENDATIONS

Mrs. Jones had one talent that eminently qualified her to do good, namely, judgment; this, even in the gay part of her life, had kept her from many mistakes; but though she had sometimes been deceived herself, she was very careful not to deceive others, by recommending people to fill any office for which they were unfit, either through selfishness or false kindness. She used to say, there is always some one appropriate quality which every person must possess, in order to fit them for any particular employment.

"Even in this quality," said she to Mr. Simpson the clergyman, "I do not expect perfection; but if they are destitute of this, whatever good qualities they may possess besides, though they may do for some other employment, they will not do for this. If I want a pair of shoes, I go to a shoemaker; I do not go to a man of another trade, however ingenious he may be, to ask him if he cannot *contrive* to make me a pair of shoes. When I lived in London, I learned to be much on my guard as to recommendations. I found people often wanted to impose on me some one who was a burden to themselves. Once, I remember, when I undertook to get a matron for an hospital, half my acquaintance had some one to offer me. Mrs. Gibson sent me an old cook, whom she herself had discharged for wasting her own provisions; yet she had the conscience to recommend this woman to take care of the provisions of a large community. Mrs. Grey sent me a discarded housekeeper, whose constitution had been ruined by sitting up with Mrs. Grey's gouty husband; but who she yet thought might do well enough to undergo the fatigue of taking care of a hundred poor sick people. A third friend sent me a woman who had no merit but that of being very poor, and it would be charity to provide for her. The truth is, the lady was obliged to allow her a small pension till she could get her off her own hands, by turning her on those of others."

"It is very true, madam," said Mr. Simpson; "the right way is always to prefer the good of the many to the good of one; if, indeed, it can be called doing good to any one, to place them in a station in which they must feel unhappy, by not knowing how to discharge the duties of it. I will tell you how I manage. If the persons recommended are objects of charity, I privately subscribe to their wants; I pity and help them; but I never promote them to a station for which they are unfit, as I should, by so doing, hurt a whole community, to help a distressed individual."

Thus Mrs. Jones resolved, that the first step towards setting up her school should be to provide a suitable mistress.

The vestry were so earnest in recommending one woman, that she
thought it worth looking into. On
inquiry, she found it was a scheme to
take a large family off the parish; they
never considered that a very ignorant
woman, with a family of young children, was, of all others, the most unfit
for a school; all they considered was,
that the profits of the school might
enable her to live without parish pay.
Mrs. Jones refused another, though she
could read well, and was decent in her
conduct, because she used to send her
children to the shop on Sundays. And
she objected to a third, a very sensible
woman, because she was suspected
of making an outward profession of
religion a cloak for immoral conduct.
Mrs. Jones knew she must not be too
nice, neither; she knew she must put
up with many faults at last.

"I know," said she to Mr. Simpson, "the imperfection of every thing that is human. As the mistress will have much to bear with from the children, so I expect to have something to bear with in the mistress; and she and I must submit to our respective trials, by thinking how much God has to bear with in us all. But there are certain qualities which are indispensable in certain situations. There are, in particular, three things which a schoolmistress must not be without—*good sense, activity*, and *piety*. Without the first, she will mislead others; without the second, she will neglect them; and without the third, though she may civilize, yet she will never Christianize them."

Mr. Simpson said, "he really knew but of one person in the parish who was fully likely to answer her purpose: this," continued he, "is no other than

my housekeeper, Mrs. Betty Crew. It
will, indeed, be a great loss to me to
part from her; and to her, it will be a
far more fatiguing life than that which
she at present leads. But ought I to put
my own personal comfort, or ought
Betty to put her own ease and quiet,
in competition with the good of above
a hundred children? This will appear
still more important, if we consider
the good done by these institutions,
not as *fruit,* but *seed;* if we take into the
account how many yet unborn may
become Christians, in consequence of
our making these children Christians;
for how can we calculate the number
which may be hereafter trained for
heaven, by those very children we are
going to teach, when they themselves
shall become parents, and you and I
are dead and forgotten? To be sure, by
parting from Betty, my pea-soup will

not be quite so well flavored, nor my linen so neatly got up; but the day is fast approaching when all this will signify but little; but it will not signify little whether one hundred immortal souls were the better from my making this petty sacrifice. Mrs. Crew is a real Christian, has excellent sense, and had a good education from my mother. She has also had a little sort of preparatory training for the business; for when the poor children come to the parsonage for broth on a Saturday evening, she is used to appoint them all to come at the same time; and after she has filled their pitchers, she ranges them round her in the garden, and examines them in their catechism. She is just and fair in dealing out the broth and beef, not making my favor to the parents depend on the skill of their children; but her own old caps, and ribands, and cast-off clothes, are bestowed as little rewards on the best scholars; so that taking the time she spends in working for them and the things she gives them, there is many a lady who does not exceed Mrs. Crew in acts of charity. This I mention to confirm your notion, that it is not necessary to be rich in order to do good; a religious upper servant has great opportunities of this sort, if the master is disposed to encourage her."

My readers, I trust, need not be informed, that this is that very Mrs. Betty Crew who assisted Mrs. Jones in teaching poor women to cut out linen, and dress cheap dishes, as related in the "The Cottage Cook." Mrs. Jones, in the following week, got together as many of the mothers as she could, and spoke to them as follows:—

MRS. JONES'S EXHORTATION

"My good women:—on Sunday next I propose to open a school for the instruction of your children. Those among you, who know what it is to be able to read your Bible, will, I doubt not, rejoice that the same blessing is held out to your children. You who are *not* able yourselves to read what your Savior has done and suffered for you, ought to be doubly anxious that your children should reap a blessing which you have lost. Would not that mother be thought an unnatural monster, who should stand by and snatch out of her child's mouth the bread which a kind friend had just put into it? But such a mother would be merciful, compared with her who should rob her children of the opportunity of learning to read the word of God when it is held

MRS. JONES RECOMMENDED GOOD BOOKS.

out to them. Remember, that if you
slight the present offer, or if, after having sent your children a few times, you
should afterwards keep them at home
under vain pretences, you will have to
answer for it at the day of judgment.
Let not your poor children, *then*, have
cause to say, 'My fond mother was my
worst enemy. I might have been bred
up in the fear of the Lord, and she

opposed it, for the sake of giving me a little paltry pleasure. For an idle holiday, I am now brought to the gates of hell!' My dear women, which of you could bear to see your darling child condemned to everlasting destruction? Which of you could bear to hear him accuse you as the cause of it? Is there any mother here present, who will venture to say, 'I will doom the child I bore to sin and hell, rather than put them or myself to a little present pain, by curtailing their evil inclinations! I will let them spend the Sabbath in ignorance and idleness, instead of rescuing them from vanity and sin, by sending them to school!' If there are any such here present, let that mother who values her child's pleasure more than his soul, now walk away, while I set down in my list the names of all those who wish to bring their young ones up in the way that leads to eternal life, instead of indulging them in the pleasures of sin, which are but for a moment."

When Mrs. Jones had done speaking, most of the women thanked her for her good advice, and hoped that God would give them grace to follow it; promising to send their children constantly. Others, who were not so well disposed, were yet afraid to refuse, after the sin of so doing had been so plainly set before them. The worst of the women had kept away from this meeting, resolving to set their faces against the school. Most of those, also, who were present, as soon as they got home, set about providing their children with what little decent apparel they could raise. Many a willing mother lent her tall daughter her hat, best cap, and white handkerchief; and

many a grateful father spared his linen
waistcoat and bettermost hat, to induce
his grown-up son to attend; for it was
a rule with which Mrs. Jones began,
that she would not receive the younger
children out of any family who did not
send their elder ones. Too many made
excuses that their shoes were old, or
their hat worn out. But Mrs. Jones told
them not to bring any excuses to her,
which they could not bring to the day
of judgment; and among those excuses,
she would hardly admit any except
accidents, sickness, or attendance on
sick parents or young children.

SUBSCRIPTIONS

Mrs. Jones, who had secured large
subscriptions from the gentry, was
desirous of getting the help and counte-
nance of the farmers and trades-people,

whose duty and interest she thought it was, to support a plan calculated to improve the virtue and happiness of the parish. Most of them subscribed, and promised to see that their workmen sent their children. She met with little opposition till she called on farmer Hoskins. She told him, as he was the richest farmer in the parish, she came to him for a handsome subscription.

"Subscription!" said he, "it is nothing but subscriptions, I think; a man had need be made of money."

"Farmer," said Mrs. Jones, "God has blessed you with abundant prosperity, and he expects you should be liberal in proportion to your great ability."

"I do not know what you mean by blessing," said he: "I have been up early and late, lived hard while I had little, and now, when I thought I had got forward in the world, what with tithes, taxes, and subscriptions, it all goes, I think."

"Mr. Hoskins," said Mrs. Jones, "as to tithes and taxes, you well know, that the richer you are, the more you pay; so that your murmurs are a proof of your wealth. This is but an ungrateful return for all your blessings."

"You are again at your blessings," said the farmer; "but let every man work as hard as I have done, and I dare say he will do as well. It is to my own industry I owe what I have. My crops have been good, because I minded my ploughing and sowing."

"O farmer!" cried Mrs. Jones, "you forget whose suns and showers make your crops to grow, and who it is that giveth strength to get riches. But I do not come to preach, but to beg."

"Well, madam, what is the subscription now? Flannel or French? or weavers, or Swiss? or a new church, or large bread, or cheap rice? or what other new whimwham, for getting the money out of one's pocket?"

"I am going to establish a Sunday school, farmer; and I come to you, as one of the principal inhabitants of the parish; hoping your example will spur on the rest to give."

"Why, then," said the farmer, "as one of the principal inhabitants of the parish, I will give nothing; hoping it will spur on the rest to refuse. Of all the foolish inventions, and new-fangled devices to ruin the country, that of teaching the poor to read is the very worst."

"And I, farmer, think that to teach good principles to the lower classes, is the most likely way to save the country. Now, in order to this, we must teach them to read."

"Not with my consent, nor my

money," said the farmer; "for I know it always does more harm than good."

"So it may," said Mrs. Jones, "if you only teach them to read, and then turn them adrift, to find out books for themselves.[1] There is a proneness in the heart to evil, which it is our duty to oppose, and which I see you are promoting. Only look round your own kitchen; I am ashamed to see it hung round with

1   It was this consideration, chiefly, which stimulated the conductors of the Cheap Repository to send forth that variety of little books so peculiarly suited to the young. They considered that, by means of Sunday schools, multitudes were now taught to read, who would be exposed to be corrupted by all the ribaldry and profaneness of loose songs, vicious stories, and, especially, by the new influx of corruption arising from Jacobinical and atheistical pamphlets; and that it was a bounden duty to counteract such temptations. *(Original footnote)*

loose songs and ballads. I grant, indeed, it would be better for your men and maids, and even your daughters, not to be able to read at all, than to read such stuff as this. But if, when they ask for bread, you will give them a stone, nay, worse, a serpent, yours is the blame." Then, taking up a penny book which had a very loose title, she went on: "I do not wonder, if you, who read such books as these, think it safer that people should not read at all."

The farmer grinned, and said, "It is hard, if a man of my substance may not divert himself; when a bit of fun costs only a penny, and a man can spare that penny, there is no harm done. When it is very hot, or very wet, and I come in to rest, and have drunk my mug of cider, I like to take up a bit of a jest-book, or a comical story, to make me laugh."

"O, Mr. Hoskins!" replied Mrs. Jones, "when you come in to rest from a burning sun, or shower, do you never think of Him whose sun it is that is ripening your corn? or whose shower is filling the ear, or causing the grass to grow? I could tell you of some books which would strengthen such thoughts, whereas such as you read only serve to put them out of your head."

Mrs. Jones having taken pains to let Mr. Hoskins know, that all the genteel and wealthy people had subscribed, he at last said, "Why, as to the matter of that, I do not value a crown; only I think it might be better bestowed; and I am afraid my own workmen will fly in my face, if once they are made scholars; and that they will think themselves too good to work."

"Now you talk soberly, and give

your reasons," said Mrs. Jones; "weak as they are, they deserve an answer. Do you think that either man, woman, or child, ever did his duty the worse, only because he knew it the better?"

"No, perhaps not."

"Now, the whole extent of learning which we intend to give the poor, is only to enable them to read the Bible; a book which brings to us the glad tidings of salvation; in which every duty is explained, every doctrine brought into practice, and the highest truths made level to the meanest understanding. The knowledge of that book, and its practical influence on the heart, is the best security you can have, both for the industry and obedience of your servants. Now, can you think any man will be the worse servant for being a good Christian?"

"Perhaps not."

"Are not the duties of children, of servants, and the poor, individually and expressly set forth in the Bible?"

"Yes."

"Do you think any duties are likely to be so well performed from any human motives, such as fear or prudence, as from those religious motives which are backed with the sanction of rewards and punishments, of heaven or hell? Even upon your own principles of worldly policy, do you think a poor man is not less likely to steal a sheep or a horse, who was taught, when a boy, that it was a sin, that it was breaking a commandment, to rob a hen-roost or an orchard, than one who has been bred in ignorance of God's law? Will your property be secured so effectually by the stocks on the green, as by teaching the boys in the school, 'that for all these things God will bring them into judgment'?[1] Is a poor fellow, who can read his Bible, so likely to sleep or to drink away his few hours of leisure, as one who *cannot* read? He may, and he often does, make a bad use of his reading; but I doubt he would have been as bad without it; and the hours spent in learning to read, will always have been among the most harmless ones of his life."

"Well, madam," said the farmer, "if you do not think that religion will spoil my young servants, I do not care if you do put me down for half a guinea. What has farmer Dobson given?"

"Half a guinea," said Mrs. Jones.

"Well," cried the farmer, "it shall never be said I do not give more than he, who is only a renter. Dobson half a guinea! Why, he wears his coat as thread-bare as a laborer."

1   Ecclesiastes 11:9.

"Perhaps," replied Mrs. Jones, "that is one reason why he gives so much."

"Well, put me down a guinea," cried the farmer; "as scarce as guineas are just now, I'll never be put upon the same footing with Dobson, neither."

"Yes, and you must exert yourself, besides, in insisting that your workmen send their children, and often look into the school yourself, to see if they are there, and reward or discourage them accordingly," added Mrs. Jones. "The most zealous teachers will flag in their exertions, if they are not animated and supported by the wealthy; and your poor youths will soon despise religious instruction as a thing forced upon them, as a hardship added to their other hardships, if it be not made pleasant by the encouraging presence, kind words, and little gratuities from their betters."

Here Mrs. Jones took her leave; the farmer insisted on waiting on her to the door. When they got into the yard, they spied Mr. Simpson, who was standing near a little group of females, consisting of the farmer's two young daughters, and a couple of rosy dairy-maids, an old blind fiddler, and a woman who led him. The woman had laid a basket on the ground, out of which she was dealing some songs to the girls, who were kneeling round it, and eagerly picking out such whose titles suited their tastes. On seeing the clergyman come up, the fiddler's companion (for I am sorry to say she was not his wife) pushed some of the songs to the bottom of the basket, turned round to the company, and, in a whining tone, asked if they would please to buy a godly book. Mr. Simpson saw through the hypocrisy at once, and, instead of making any answer, took out of one of the girls' hands a song, which the woman had not been able to snatch away. He was shocked and grieved to see that these young girls were about to read, to sing, and to learn by heart, such ribaldry as he was ashamed even to cast his eyes on. He turned about to the girl, and gravely, but mildly, said, "Young woman, what do you think should be done to a person who should be found carrying a box of poison round the country, and leaving a little at every house?"

The girls all agreed that such a person ought to be hanged.

"That he should," said the farmer, "if I was upon the jury, and quartered too."

The fiddler and his woman were of the same opinion; declaring, *they* would not do such a wicked thing for the world, for if they were poor they were honest. Mr. Simpson, turning to the other girl, said, "Which is of most value, the soul or the body?"

"The soul, sir," said the girl. "Why so?" said he.

"Because, sir, I have heard you say, in the pulpit, the soul is to last forever."

"Then," cried Mr. Simpson, in a stern voice, turning to the fiddler's woman, "Are you not ashamed to sell poison for that part which is to last forever? poison for the soul?"

"Poison!" said the terrified girl, throwing down the book, and shuddering as people do who are afraid they have touched something infectious.

"Poison!" echoed the farmer's daughter, recollecting with horror the ratsbane which Lion, the old housedog, had got at the day before, and after eating which, she had seen him drop down dead in convulsions.

"Yes," said Mr. Simpson to the woman, "I do again repeat, the souls of these innocent girls will be poisoned, and may be eternally ruined, by this vile trash which you carry about."

"I now see," said Mrs. Jones to the farmer, "the reason why you think learning to read does more harm than good. It is indeed far better that they should never know how to tell a letter, unless you keep such trash as this out of the way, and provide them with what is good, or at least what is harmless. Still this is not the fault of reading, but the abuse of it. Wine is still a good cordial, though it is too often abused to the purpose of drunkenness."

The farmer said that neither of his maids could read their horn-book, though he owned he often heard them singing that song which the parson thought so bad, but for his part it made him as merry as a nightingale.

"Yes," said Mrs. Jones, "as a proof that it is not merely being able to read which does the mischief, I have often heard, as I have been crossing a hayfield, young girls singing such indecent ribaldry as has driven me out of the field, though I well knew they could not read a line of what they were singing, but had caught it from others. So, you see, you may as well say the memory is a wicked talent because some people misapply it, as to say that reading is dangerous because some folks abuse it."

While they were talking, the fiddler and his woman were trying to steal away unobserved, but Mr. Simpson stopped them, and sternly said, "Woman, I shall have some further talk with you. I am a magistrate, as well as a minister; and, if I know it, I will no more allow a wicked book to be sold in my parish than a dose of poison."

The girls threw away all their songs, thanked Mr. Simpson, begged Mrs. Jones would take them into her school after they had done milking in the evenings, that they might learn to read only what was proper. They promised they would never more deal with any but sober, honest hawkers, such as sell good little books, Christmas carols, and harmless songs, and desired the fiddler's woman never to call there again.

This little incident afterwards confirmed Mrs. Jones in a plan she had before some thoughts of putting in practice. This was, after her school had been established a few months, to invite all the well-disposed grown-up youth of the parish to meet her at the school an hour or two on a Sunday evening, after the necessary business of the dairy, and of serving the cattle, was over. Both Mrs. Jones and her agent had the talent of making this time pass so agreeably, by their manner of explaining Scripture, and of impressing the heart by serious and affectionate discourse, that in a short time the evening-school was nearly filled with a second company, after the younger ones were dismissed. In time, not only the servants, but the sons and daughters of the most substantial people in the parish, attended. At length, many of the parents, pleased with the improvement so visible in the young people, got a habit of dropping in, that they might learn how to instruct their own families. And it was observed, that as the school filled, not only the five's-court and public-house were thinned, but even Sunday gossiping and tea-visiting declined. Even farmer Hoskins, who was at first angry with his maids for leaving off those *merry* songs (as he called them), was so pleased by the manner in which the psalms were sung at the school, that he promised Mrs. Jones to make her a present of half a sheep towards her first Mayday feast. Of this feast, and some further account of the Sunday school, see the History of Hester Wilmot, in a future Part.

About the Author

HANNAH MORE (1745-1833) was born in Stapleton, Bristol, England. Her father was a school headmaster and she had four outgoing sisters. She had three failed engagements to the same man Edward Turner, who settled with an annuity for her trouble, and she remained unmarried. Early in her life she was interested in the theater and wrote plays. Dr. James Stonhouse (also the vicar in *Shepherd of Salisbury Plain*) introduced her to David Garrick, a theater owner, who produced her work in the theater.

For six years her fashionable social life grew to include many important people, but when it lost its appeal she turned to religion. Dr. James Stonhouse is credited with Hannah More's spiritual awakening, but it was

John Newton's influence that gave energy and devotion to her spiritual walk, and she became a strong evangelical Christian.

Education was a strong theme in her life and William Wilberforce encouraged her to start schools, for the education and moral advancement of poor village children.

To counteract immoral forces in society, Hannah More, her sister Sarah, and others wrote a series of successful chapbooks called the "Cheap Repository Tracts." These included the *Shepherd of Salisbury Plain* and many other colorful tales.

She was also active with a group called the "Clapham Sect" that met at Henry Thornton's huge house in Clapham. They included William Wiberforce, Henry Venn, James Stephen, Zachary McCauley, Thomas

Gisborne, and Charles Grant. They met for the reformation of society.

The last part of her life was at Barley Wood, where she continued her goals of education and moral improvement. She had a vast social circle and wrote a multitude of letters. Her talent for writing produced many books of drama, poetry, hymns, fiction and religious instruction.

About this Book

MRS. JONES learns that "going about and doing good" would lift her spirits and would cost nothing. She became a good Samaritan and helped keep the village merchants honest. The "cottage cook" set up a school to teach villagers how to save money by cooking at home and other household skills.

In the "Sunday School," Mrs. Jones explains about her school and details the problems of finding a good school mistress. She exhorts people to read good books and explains the importance of Christian behavior.

The Advertisement for the Cheap Repository Tracts

TO IMPROVE the habits, and raise the principles of the common people, at a time when their dangers and temptations, moral and political, were multiplied beyond the example of any former period, was the motive which impelled the Author of these volumes to devise and prosecute the institution of the Cheap Repository. This plan was established with an humble wish, not only to counteract vice and profligacy on the one hand, but error, discontent, and false religion, on the other. And as an appetite for reading had, from a variety of causes, been increasing among the inferior ranks in this country, it was judged expedient, at this critical period, to supply such wholesome aliment as might give a new direction to their taste, and abate their relish for those corrupt and inflammatory publications which the consequences of the French revolution have been so fatally pouring in upon us.

The success of the plan exceeded the most sanguine expectation of its projector. Above two millions of the tracts were sold within the first year, besides very large numbers in Ireland; and they continue to be very, extensively circulated, in their original form of single pieces, and also in three bound volumes.

As these stories, though *principally* are not calculated *exclusively* for the middle and lower classes of society, the Author has, at the desire of her friends, selected those which were written by herself, and presented them to the public.

Man's Questions & God's Answers

Am I accountable to God?
Each of us will give an account of himself to God.
ROMANS 14:12 (NIV).

Has God seen all my ways?
*Everything is uncovered and laid bare before the eyes
of him to whom we must give account.*
HEBREWS 4:13 (NIV).

Does he charge me with sin?
*But the Scripture declares that the whole world is a
prisoner of sin.* GALATIANS 3:22 (NIV).
All have sinned and fall short of the glory of God.
ROMANS 3:23 (NIV).

Will he punish sin?
The soul who sins is the one who will die.
EZEKIEL 18:4 (NIV).
*For the wages of sin is death, but the gift of God is
eternal life in Christ Jesus our Lord.*
ROMANS 6:23 (NIV).

Must I perish?
*He is patient with you, not wanting anyone to perish,
but everyone to come to repentance.*
2 PETER 3:9 (NIV).

How can I escape?
Believe in the Lord Jesus, and you will be saved.
ACTS 16:31 (NIV).

Is he able to save me?

Therefore he is able to save completely those who come to God through him. HEBREWS 7:25 (NIV).

Is he willing?

Christ Jesus came into the world to save sinners. 1 TIMOTHY 1:15 (NIV).

Am I saved on believing?

Whoever believes in the Son has eternal life, but whoever rejects the Son will not see life, for God's wrath remains on him. JOHN 3:36 (NIV).

Can I be saved now?

Now is the time of God's favor, now is the day of salvation. 2 CORINTHIANS 6:2 (NIV).

As I am?

Whoever comes to me I will never drive away. JOHN 6:37 (NIV).

Shall I not fall away?

Him who is able to keep you from falling. JUDE 1:24 (NIV).

If saved, how should I live?

Those who live should no longer live for themselves but for him who died for them and was raised again. 2 CORINTHIANS 5:15 (NIV).

What about death and eternity?

I am going there to prepare a place for you. I will come back and take you to be with me that you also may be where I am. JOHN 14:2-3 (NIV).

Made in United States
Orlando, FL
02 May 2023